*Donated
in
Memory of*

KAY JOHNSON

A Bite of Black History

Beatrice Garrett

Copyright © 1992 by Beatrice Garrett

First printing 1992

Library of Congress Cataloging-in-Publication Data

Garrett, Beatrice
      A Bite of Black History
ISBN   09629887-1-5 : $14.95

Books available at special discounts for bulk purchases,
sales promotions, fund-raising or educational use.
For details, contact

Sales Director
Bosck Publishing House
P.O. Box 2311
Los Angeles, Calif. 90051-0311

Printed in the United States of America   CIP 91-74117

This book is dedicated to my children
CRYSTAL, SHAWN, KENYA AND OMAR
and to all my friends and relatives who
encouraged me along the way... but especially
for my mother and father
ROOSEVELT and LORETTA GLASCO

Poems in this book appeared in the following publications to which acknowledgement and thanks are made;

Los Angeles Sentinel newspaper; THE BEARS' TALE, Livingston College, Salisbury, N.C.; Clark College, Creative Writing Award, Atlanta, Georgia; THE LAMP, Florida Memorial College, Miami, Florida; INNERVISIONS and BLACK STUDENT UNION, Trade Technical College, Los Angeles, California; DAWN MAGAZINE, Baltimore, Maryland; COMMUNITY CLIPPER PUBLICATIONS, Los Angeles, California; BLACK HOLLYWOOD MAGAZINE, Los Angeles, California; THE NEW WRITER'S GUILD, Los Angeles, California.

A special thanks to Susan Cooper, who patiently and enthusiastically typed my work with no ado...

A very special thanks to POETRY ATLANTA who kept the adrenalin flowing.

Preface

I hope that my small contribution to Afro-American history will whet the appetite of all young readers enough for them to want to explore and research further this most important integral part of American history known as slavery. This "peculiar institution" was methodically deleted from the text-books in our school system and by doing so excluded the tremendous contributions that our Black ancestors made who were instrumental in making this country one of the richest nations in the world. This national greatness was perpetuated by inhuman bartering tyrants who reaped the benefits of this free labor relief called slavery.

The students of America have been shackled with stereotypes, myths, hatred and discrimination because the truth of the matter has been covered with a blanket of disguise, mistrust, hatred, deception and fraud.

History is supposed to be a factual record of chronological events that are not hidden, watered-down or deleted. When this country makes up its mind to present American history in its fullest entirety, then we can began to hope for a better relationship and understanding for each other.

B.G.

*"If it's too deep,
dont' go in the water"*

Table of Contents

Forty Acres and a Mule

The Civil War is over,
And you've set black folks free.
The peace between the North and South
Will go down in history.
But I am here to tell you
That there's something you forgot:
What happened to my forty acres
And a mule?

Now, please don't think I'm ungrateful
For this freedom that you gave.
You were only trying to make amends
For making black folks your slave.
But you gave us all a promise,
And I hope this one comes true.
I need my forty acres
And a mule.

You made other people promises,
Paid them off with great rewards.
Now, I'm not jealous of that fact,
And I'm happy for their cause.
But I've worked for you in slavery,
And I've paid my dues in full,
And I want my forty acres
And a mule!

Did you take my forty acres,
And sign it away with the mule?
Did you take advantage of black folks
That never went to school?
You said we took off running,
Didn't stay to get our claim.
What happened to my forty acres
And a mule?

Some people want to be snooty,
And forget about the past.
But I want everything that belongs to me,
Including my land and my ass.
Don't pat me on the shoulder and say,
"Tomorrow's another day."
You'd better give me my forty acres
And a mule!

The years are passing swiftly,
And folks are getting old.
Some have died and even cried
That the white man was so cold.
But I am here to tell you,
No matter how long it takes,
I'm going to get my forty acres
And a mule!

Black Cargo

Black cargo was the bill of fare,
And I in my prime a young girl there,
In bracelets of iron on hands and feet
Taken from my home in bartered discreet.
Such were my years, maybe twelve and ten,
A young girl captured I knew not when.
The years escape me but I knew then
That fate had dealt me a terrible hand
With unpaid passage to a distant land.

Giant slave ships moored on the Ivory Coast,
Awaiting their bounty from the trader's post
While crewmen prompted us to the sandy shore
And I knew I would see my land no more.
As I fell and kissed the copper sand
And the grains slipped quickly through my hands,
Warm tears bathed my wind-blown face
And I prayed to my God for redeeming grace.
I was a slave!

With naked bodies we stood packed in the hold,
Stacked books of flesh to be sold for gold.
Only shackles and chains would be my wed
And I knew by the range there would be no bed.
Only wooden planks and foul air to breath.
How could we live when we were so deceived?
Victims of the scourge of white man's hate,
Migrated to a land of unknown fate.
Yes, I was there!

And yes, the road of fate was paved
With unknown evils of hate and rage.
A road of whips and chains and hemp;
Black men and women held in contempt.
While heartless men with gleaming eyes
Counted one by one their bounty prize
Of human chattel and merchandise,
I prayed each day that I would die!

3

But no, sweet death would not beckon me;
A vengeful power had its victory.
No victuals would I eat aboard that ship,
But the Captain's speculum pried open my lips
With hate and lust from demonic eyes,
I knew they would not let me die.
Those torturous instruments of sadistic men
Who knew how to make a young girl bend
And yes, I cried!

And the raging winds and rain and heat
Pierced like a knife of avenging feat.
As the great ship plowed on wind-born spree
Through the deep dark bowels of the Atlantic sea,
As the towering waves fluxed its overflow,
The Captain veered both sharks and foe
With great guns trained on the decks below,
To protect his value of black cargo,
We were his prize!

And yes, the days did come and go,
And many had died on the decks below.
The stench of death and disease in the air,
I remember it well with great despair.
Some took their lives as well they should,
I too would pass if only I could.
For only death would set me free,
Since this life of mine had no guarantee.

You could not know, you were not there,
How I cried to God in humble despair
To take this cup of bitter myrrh
And end my life upon this earth.
With a piercing stab from a crewman's knife
I had the chance to take my life.
With the smile of freedom upon my lips,
I knew I could leave this wretched ship!

There will be no brand upon my breast,
No work for me until I sweat.
No gleaning in the field of life,
Or torturous hell of pain and strife.
I will never breed on a slaver's farm,
Bear children to be taken from my arms.
Or share the white man's lustful bed,
While my husband hangs his shameful head!

And I will never feel the hangman's rope
Or cry when I know there is no hope.
Or smell the stench of burning flesh
Or lose the ones that I love best.
There will never be the flogger's whip,
Or perpetual change of ownership.
No "steal away" by the moonlit sky,
For a better life in the by and by.

And to those who write the history books
With slanted truths and views with hooks,
Let them tell the story still untold
Of a young girl's life that did not unfold.
Who knew greed and lust and tyranny
And who chose a death and not slavery.
This young girl in this anguished time,
A victim of the cruelest kind.

And yes, the ships are sailing still,
Taking black men and women against their will.
To a land where cries of "Liberty"
Mean nothing at all to those not free.
While the great ships plowed on a wind-born spree,
Through the deep dark bowels of the Atlantic sea,
And the Captain's eyes gleam demonically,
And I cried, "Oh God! Have mercy on me,"
I won my prize!

Moving Around

I've been bought and sold so many times,
Don't know if I'm coming or going.
To Master Grace and Master Pace
And then to Master Owens.
As soon as I set my gunnysack down
And look around the place,
As sure as day, I'm on my way,
Because I have been replaced.
They get a heaping price for me,
Each time the bidding gets higher.
But that don't help me none at all,
I get more ruffled and tired.
If I could lay down my weary head,
And put my shoes up under a bed,
I'd do my work and be well behaved,
At least until they free the Slaves.

Dr. Mary McLeod Bethune
(1875-1955)

She walked the road
Of accomplishments,
Her sight on
Black education.
A stately woman
With great intent,
Preparing for a
New generation.
She founded a college
With her tenacity,
Taught the art of
Faith, love and charity.
A civil rights leader
For great presidents,
Her head held high,
She never bent.
With medals of honor
For all to see,
This proud black woman
Helped set us free.
A precious gift
From a kindred mind,
Her memory will last
Until the end of time.

Pot Liquor

The slaves survived on pot liquor,
The juice from the collard greens.
They drank it when there was no meat
Or any food at all to eat.
They poured it over cornmeal mush
And fed the babies that good stuff.
When Mama cooks a mess of greens
It takes so long, or so it seems.
If people took the time to think,
They'd never pour pot liquor down the sink.

Slave Poetress
Phillis Wheatley (1753-1784)

Oh, gentle muse of African flair,
Such sparkling eyes and raven hair.
A chattel of such rebel times,
God's hallowed heir of love sublime.
Ingenious words on sacred wings
Acclaimed by generals, poets and kings.
Such "poems on various subjects" loved,
A burning creed from heaven above.
Pray tell black goddess who inspired
Such tapestry from Parnassian's Lyre?
Majestic halls grant jubilee
For tireless throngs in history.

Juneteenth
(June 19th)

Juneteenth is a holiday
The descendants of slaves celebrate.
Some states let the slaves keep working
Long after their freedom day.
No one told the slaves they were free;
It would interfere with the economy.
So the slaves worked on not knowing their fate.
Juneteenth is the day that they celebrate
Their freedom...

The Railroad

Free labor on the railroad tracks,
Work so hard we break our backs.
Busting rocks and laying tracks,
Don't look up and don't look back.
Free labor on the railroad tracks,
White man driving, that's a fact.
Got to get up before the morning sun,
White man wants his railroad done.
Free labor on the railroad tracks,
Hear that whip lash crack, crack, crack,
Laid so hard upon your back,
Got to hurry and lay those tracks,
Free labor on the railroad tracks,
Sun so hot it makes you black.
Sweating bullets down your back,
You get no money, and that's a fact.

The Sable Genius
Benjamin Banneker (1731-1806)

Free-born Negro in his time,
Wrapped in his cloak of knowledge,
Studying the glittering stars.
Essayist, inventor, and mathematician.
The mind of a genius.

The *Banneker Almanac;*
Lover of phenomena and truth
In scientific pursuit.
Inventor of the wooden clock.
A planner of our nation's capitol.
The eyes of a genius.

Studying the bees and locusts;
A prophet of hidden energies.
A hater of slavery's ills;
Entwined in the sequel of life.
Lover of man and peace.
The heart of a genius.

My Wish

If I could only read and write
And understand the things I read;
To see the characters on the page,
And know all of my ABC's.

To write down all my inner thoughts
And see them written on a page;
To read and write like others do,
This is my wish, but I'm a Slave.

To hold a book up to my eyes
And see the hidden treasures there,
And travel over land and sea,
And end up almost anywhere.

Oh, sacred fire of my desire,
It's been so long, my time is due.
If I could only read and write
And have my share of freedom, too.

Thirty-Nine Lashes

Thirty-nine lashes
With a cowskin whip;
Laid on our backs,
Laid on our hips.
Punishment for things
We did not do;
Punishment to last
The whole year through.
Thirty-nine lashes
And maybe more,
Kept us in bondage
And doing our chores.

Love Songs
Antar (615 A.D.)

Black mother's son
From Arabic fire,
Kindred flames from
Poet's lyre.

Odes of beauty
From a land of love,
Melodic words of
Love's desire.

Your voice on wings
Set to inspire
Such joyous words
Of ecstasy.

Oh, ancient warrior
Your gift of love
Retains the world
Throughout eternity.

Come On

You want my son, then
Come and get him,
Over my dead body if you can.
You said he stole a ham and chicken:
Is that enough to kill a man?
My gun is cocked and loaded, Mister,
I'll blow the socks off your feet.
I birth this child and yes, I know him,
And won't stand to see him mistreat.
Don't take my word, just come in closer,
You'll meet your Maker down the line,
I'm standing with the barrel loaded,
Finger triggered and you're going to die!

Crumbs

Looking for crumbs
From the white man's table,
Looking for crumbs to eat.
Crumbs don't last long,
Or make you able,
And crumbs don't set you free.

Full Moon

The Full Moon looked down
On the runaway Slaves
And wondered what he could do.
"I'll brighten my light
And pave the way
And call on the others, too."
He beckoned the Wind
To roll back the clouds
And quiet the storms,
At least for awhile.
Then asked the North Star
To point the way
To make the sky as bright as day.
"We'll work together secretly
Until every runaway is free."

The Runaways

They left in dead of night
By small and narrow paths,
Not knowing where to go
Some at the hands of wrath.

Those helpless wretched slaves
Who labored long with time,
Not knowing what to do
Had freedom on their mind.

Some left with so much fear
For loved ones left behind.
They dread the clanging chains
With hound dogs on the line.

Some wanted to return
But knew within their hearts
That they would pay the price
With death their counterpart.

Their bodies dressed in rags,
No shoes upon their feet,
Through storms and wind and hail
And sometimes burning heat.

They found refuge by day
Along the wooded swamps.
Made forest floors their bed
To keep them safe from harm.

They had that one bright star
To guide them on their way.
Some feared the darkness so,
But they would kneel and pray.

They prayed that God would soothe
Their hunger pangs and thirst,
And show them how to live
On blessings from the Earth.

And yes the feat was great
A case of life or death,
But faith would be their steer
With each and every breath.

Some died along the way
With freedom on their lips.
In watery graves they lay,
So short their freedom trip.

What did they hope to find
These children of the night?
Their freedom from all fear
And yes, their civil rights.

Oh slaves, what faith you had
To walk with the unknown.
Your God did light the path
Which found your freedom home.

Paul Laurence Dunbar
(1892-1906)

A bard who left
The gift of verse,
Whom some accepted
And others shirked.
Preserving our dialect
So lyrically,
Held national prominence
In American poetry.
A product of
Pure African blood,
Who wrote of laughter,
Sympathy and love.
A merry heart on a
Sorrowful scene,
His life was brief but
He fulfilled his dream.

Let's Talk

There are many things
We could talk about;
Let's talk about
Black History instead.
Some things remembered,
Some forgot,
Some things better
Left unsaid.

It's too late to talk about the shackles,
And the maiming and chaining, too,
Or the naked bodies that froze in the cold,
And the ones that walked with no shoes.

No need to talk about the lashings,
Or the lynch ropes in cruel white hands,
Or the endless toiling in the cotton fields;
These things keep you from taking a stand.

I won't even talk about the times
There was hunger and no food to eat,
Except corn meal mush and water,
And bones that had no meat.

No need to mention the leaky tin roofs
That some of us had over our heads,
As the cold wind blew in the early morn,
And some of us woke up dead.

I'm not going to get upset and moan
About black babies that starved to death;
And the mothers cried all night long,
Because they had a white baby at their breast.

Why should I bring up all these ugly things?
They are all a part of the past;
How the white man used the black woman,
And her husband was afraid to ask.

I don't even think I should define
How young boys were castrated and bled;
Because they looked at a white woman,
That was a "crime," so they said.

I won't talk about the children
Who were snatched from their mother's arms,
And separated from their families
To be worked to death on some farm.

I'm sure it won't help any
To talk about black men in chains,
Who built this country brick by brick,
And were told they had no brains.

No need to get upset about the fact
That it was a crime to read and write.
To be caught with a book was a dangerous thing;
You were taking a chance with your life.

Would it help any to point out
How black men yearned to be free?
Or how they invented many things
Without a mention in history?

Did you know about black men in prisons
Accused of crimes they didn't do?
Or the one's who were hanged and buried
With no one to come to their rescue?

Maybe I shouldn't even tell you
About the sharecroppers and their fears;
How they were never able to get out of debt,
But stayed in bondage year after year.

Did I mention the segregation?
In public places we could not go.
The trains, buses, restaurants and parks
Were run by old "Jim Crow."

Maybe it's not the time to talk about
The progress we made with closed doors;
How survival became the password,
And our ancestors prayed to the Lord.

You've been listening to me all this time,
And still you don't know my name.
I'm a proud black woman who knows the past,
Who has been watching the white man's game!

The Hanging Tree

The hanging tree near Gulcher's Creek
With branches hanging low,
Pronounced the death of those black souls
And stopped the blood that flowed.

A tree that stood with innocence
Not knowing how to move,
But bowed instead with aching heart
With deeds that were reproved.

Oh, tree of life which God bestowed,
Let not your heart be filled;
You could not stop the hangman's noose
Or save the blood that spilled.

You held the noose of angry men
Who had no love or creed.
With sad and angry arms outstretched
Deplored their foolish deeds.

The hangman's noose is put away,
But still you're full of tears.
For those who died such tragic deaths
For over a hundred years.

Tired

I'm so tired
Of all these white folks
And their secondhand
Hand-me-downs,
Worn out shoes,
And faded dresses,
While they strut
In fine silk gowns.
Lord, I know somewhere
There's nice clothes
With thin lace and
Fine silk threads.
I just hope one day
I'll wear some
Long before I end up
Dead...

A Great Man

There walked a man upon this Earth
Who touched so many lives.
He shed so many anguished tears
And hurt so deep inside.
Not a man of great beginnings;
Not a man of pompous state;
But a simple man who gave his life
And whose works were truly great.

He had a dream that one great day
Man's hatred would turn to love.
All men would live in a freedom land
And peace would reign like a dove.
Not with hatred or oppression;
Not with malice or bigotry;
But a color-blind of all mankind
With freedom and liberty.

This man became a beacon light
In a tunnel of dark despair.
A warrior who knew no hate,
In a battle that knew no fear.
Not with bullets of insurrection;
Not with weapons of hostile recourse;
But with dignity he set men free
With the silence of his soul force.

He sought a truth for all to see
In his struggle for all mankind.
A symbol of courage, hope and pain
He laid his life down on the line.
Not for treasures or fame and glory;
Not for laurels or pots of gold;
But for brotherhood he firmly stood
On his threshold of justice bold.

And then one day they struck this man
With the bullets of hate and rage.
This warrior lost the battle of life,
But won the war on our history page.
Now we sing in all his glory;
Now we sing, "Let freedom ring"
For a loving man who walked this land
Whose name was Martin Luther King.

How Many

How many arrived?
How many tied?
How many cried?
How many revived?
How many deprived?
How many thrived?
How many survived?
How many died?
You should know, you're holding the whip!

The Amistad Revolt
Joseph Cinque (1811-1879)

Joseph Cinque, an African prince
Was captured and sold for gold
Aboard the old ship "Amistad;"
With slaves he was placed in the hold.

The slave ship, in a dreadful storm,
Made possbile their skew...
With machete and knives they took
The lives of the captain and the crew.

They spared the lives of two white men
To navigate their course,
But smart these men in their revenge
sailed opposite in recourse.

Instead of touching Africa's shore,
Set sail to a Long Island port,
Cinque was captured with his men
To await their day in court.

But fate was kind in abolutionist time,
And the courts did free these men.
"Not mutineers or killers," they ruled
Because they were kidnapped then.

And so Cinque and the other slaves
Were put on a ship at hand.
With justice bend, they were all free men
To return to their native land.

Remembrance

It's hard for me to remember
How many times I kneeled and prayed,
For simple things, not diamond rings,
Just for that freedom day.
It's easy for me to remember
That freedom never came;
My whole life spent in bondage...
Were all my prayers in vain?

Freedom's Prayer

Oh, to purchase my sweet freedom.
Oh, to walk in freedom's light.
Unchained thoughts and unchained shackles,
Free me from my dreadful plight.

Light the path that leads to freedom.
Take me by your unseen hands.
Quench my thirst with pearls of wisdom.
Lead me to the Promised Land.

Melt the hardened chains of hatred.
Pluck the greed from every man.
Bound the works of Satan's pleasure
With a waving, wandering hand.

Soothe me with the balm of Gilead.
Cleanse my feet from slavery's clay.
Lay me down on your sweet bosom.
Only you can lead the way.

Gracious Savior, God Almighty,
On my bended knees I pray
For that morn of great redemption
When all men bow and must obey.

Freedom Day

Emancipation Proclamation
Finally came around.
You never saw such shouting;
Some prayed and kissed the ground.
This meant the end of slavery
And negroes were set free.
All the shouting and crying
Meant they had their liberty.
Slaves working in the cotton fields
Threw their hoes upon the ground,
For freedom meant the end of toil,
Slave barriers all knocked down.
The slaves up in the "Big House"
Looked on with great alarm.
To leave the master's comfort
Would surely bring them harm.
Some praised the name of Lincoln
For holding to his word.
They said he was a Godsend,
At least that's what they heard.
They prayed so hard for freedom,
And now that it was here,
Their hopes were for a better life,
But they were full of fear.
They feared the darkened future.
They feared the white man's wrath.
They feared the lonely road ahead.
They feared the freedom path.
Some slaves were truly hampered,
They could not read or write,
And didn't know which way to turn,
To the left or to the right.
They had no carts or horses,
Just the clothes upon their backs,
But they bundled up their children
And walked down that dusty track.

They sang their songs of freedom,
They held their heads up high.
They sang their songs of praises
As they looked up to the sky.
Look down that path to freedom,
Look down that dusty road.
Look deep into the hearts of bonded men
With freedom and no place to go.
How strange the way was opened,
How strange with unseen hands.
No burden of hate could conquer faith
As they marched on to Freedom Land.

Dr. Charles Richard Drew
(1904-1950)

The world should love you, Dr. Drew
Many lives were saved because of you.
Your research in the preservation of blood
Saved so many lives of those we love.
Yet a fatal accident took your life;
You needed blood, but were denied that right.
We shall never forget that deadly night
When you needed blood and lost your life.
Your work is still sustained—
You did not die in vain.

Slavery

I'm as old as ancient history,
And I rule with tyranny.
I've maimed and killed two million souls
In American history.
I've planned it quite precisely
As you can clearly see,
And anyone who sees me
Knows my name is Slavery.

I've kept black folks in bondage
For three hundred years or more;
Took them from their native land
And brought them to my shores.
I've starved and beat and brutalized
Both young and old, you see.
I'm a peculiar institution
Known as American Slavery.

I've tortured helpless bondsmen;
Blinded them with hurt and pain,
And worked their fingers to the bone
All free of charge and gain.
I had to fill my treasure chest
For a better life for me,
And if you're watching closely
Call me profit Slavery.

I've burned and buried humans
Without a touch of shame,
And yes, I've hanged so many men
And some were not to blame.
I've bought and sold black bodies
When they've ceased to profit me.
If you're wondering what to call me,
Call me savage Slavery.

I've branded slaves like cattle,
Used the whip to inflict pain.
Hired the bloodhound's vicious tactics
To confront the runaways.
I've conducted trials of violence
At a nearby hanging tree,
And I'll go down in history
As oppressive Slavery.

I've mused, abused and even used
The women of the lot,
And fathered bastard children
To increase the human crop.
Don't act surprised and then surmise,
Just look around and see;
I'm the father of corruption
Known as social Slavery.

I've separated families,
Strewn them all across the land.
Who cares about their problems
Or if they're ever seen again.
I'm out for mere destruction
As you can plainly see,
And if it's any comfort,
Call me inhuman Slavery.

They call me by peculiar names;
Most people think I'm dead.
But I'm behind the veil of time
Waiting to show my ugly head.
Don't be surprised if I should rise
To repeat my history:
To regain my crown of world renown
Great King of Slavery!

Old Gunny Sack

Old Gunny Sack bags,
We want to thank you;
Never had no clothes before.
We made shirts, skirts,
Pants and jackets,
And mattress covers galore,
Curtains, pillows, blankets and sheets;
Without you we would freeze to death.
In our sleep
If it wasn't for cornmeal and flour bags,
We would freeze to death in nothing but rags.

Slave Mother

There were times when I was happy,
Although locked in slaver's chains,
Looking at my baby tender,
Eyes that met in sweet exchange.
Times when all the trees were bearing
Sweet fruit kissed by the Master's hand;
Blades of green grass gently blowing
On a sea of fertile land.

Just to see the sun each morning,
Watching how the young birds fly,
And the floating clouds above me
In a bed of blue laced sky.
Watching births of new beginnings,
Seeing all God's creatures grow,
And the soft winds gently blowing,
Or the falling glistening snow.

Bubbling brooks of clear cool water,
Low green valleys near mountain tops,
Flowers blooming in the sunlight
Dressed in gowns of moist dew drops.
Flirting bees collecting sweetness,
Kissing flowers they all know,
And the rainbow with it's promise
That my God will not let go.

There were times when I was happy
And no hate could penetrate,
Feeling all of my God's glory
Standing at the Pearly Gates.
Twinkling stars light up the darkness
Telling me He's on his throne,
And the promise that He gave me
That one day I'll soon come home.

Marcus A. Garvey
(1887-1940)

He wanted dignity for his people
So far ahead of his time
Some hated and mistrusted him
But remember ignorance is blind

A trailblazer of independence
A champion of racial pride
An orator of great concern
Who founded the Black Star Ship Line

"Return to our mother country
Leave this ignorance behind
Establish your identity
Get on board the Black Star Ship Line"

But his dreams were finally broken
He was stripped of all his pride
Unjustly tried and sentenced
With a broken heart he died

Mama's Cooking

Mama's cooking
Can't be beat.
Young sweet collards
Cooked with pig's feet.
Golden brown pancakes
On the grill.
Smelling all up
And down the hill.
Fresh baked ham,
Decorated with cloves.
Candied yams
That go up your nose.
Steamed neckbones
Cooked with stringbeans;
Smothered cabbage,
Cooked with strip o' lean.
Light fluffy rolls,
So golden brown,
Melt in your mouth,
Just go to town.
Golden brown duck,
Dried out so nice,
Served with lima beans
And steamed wild rice.
Hot Apple Pie,
Ice cream on top.
Plenty to drink
Of red soda pop.
Turkey dressing
Filled with sage.
Fresh sausage patties,
Onions and eggs.
Black-eyed peas
Cooked with rice.

Mama's fixing the table
So neat and nice.
Sweet potato pie
With slices thick.
Hot cross buns
You eat so quick.
Deep dish peach cobbler,
Like Grandma used to make,
Hashed brown potatoes
With smothered steak.
Barbeque baked beans,
Texas style.
Brown, smoked ribs;
Come stay awhile.
Sit down to the table
And pull up a chair.
Once you sit down,
You ain't going nowhere!

Work

No lack of work on the plantation,
No unemployment lines,
No lunch breaks or vacation,
And you'd better get to work on time.
No sick leave or insurance,
No pay for overtime,
No laid-off notice in your box,
Work hard but you won't get a dime.
No fringe benefits or retirement,
No union dues to pay,
No forty hour week or holidays,
Keep working, you'll be free one day.
For three hundred years you worked like a mule;
For three hundred years nonstop.
If you can't work and carry your load,
You'll end up on the auction block.

Black Mother

Black Mother of the universe,
Your roots so deep within the Earth.
Few poets ever wrote of you,
The drums of life are your virtue.

Upon this Earth you shed your seed,
Through anguish, hate and lust and greed.
Through winds of war and cotton fields
Your faith was strong, you did not yield.

You strengthened unity with family ties,
Taught God and love and sacrifice;
Held all the babies at your breast
Without a sign of bitterness.

Black Mother, you are a priceless gem
Who nurtured the minds of great black men;
Instilled within us self-esteem,
And helped us hold on to our dreams.

Your lofty head held high in faith,
A solid rock on the battlefield of hate.
With God in charge at your right hand,
You're a tribute to life, a tribute to man.

Black Mother there are no laurels for you,
But the chronicle of life must deem this true:
Your love and hope and piety
Helped shape the course of destiny.

The Slave Master

Protect me, Master, from the cold,
And starve me to death inside.
Give me a few clothes to cover my back,
But lash my old black hide.

Let me work in your big white house,
But sleep in a cabin bare.
Purchase me at the Slave Market,
And sell me to those who don't care.

Teach me not to steal and lie,
But exploit me and use me, too.
You saved me from a "Savage Land;"
Can't read or write 'cause of you.

Give me the protection of your power,
But strip me of all my rights.
The things you do, I don't understand,
Because I'm black and you are white.

Malcolm X
(1925-1965)

This man became a master force
In the saga of our history.
A man some hated and some admired
Who shaped the course of destiny.
A man who walked with a passionate theme;
A fighting man some called extreme.
He taught us to hold on to our dreams,
This man called Malcolm X.

He was caught up in the struggle of time
And was so grossly misunderstood.
While slings and arrows pierced his heart,
He stood only for right and good.
"Be accountable for your life and history,
Without knowledge you lose your identity."
A praise to this man of responsibility,
This man called Malcolm X.

He said we must always take a stand,
Be proud and walk with dignity.
"We were not always slaves, you see,
But descendents of great kings and queens."
We must stick together in unity;
Without each other, we will never be free.
He taught us hope, love and charity,
This man called Malcolm X.

He walked across the stage of life
Caught up in a terrible hell.
A soldier of truth and self-esteem,
But too soon the curtain fell.
His plans and dreams would never be,
But he opened our eyes so we might see.
This precious gift of our legacy,
This man called Malcolm X.

How Many Times?

How many bales of cotton
You got to pick to make a dime?
How many rows you got to hoe
In this one miserable lifetime?
How many winters you got to freeze?
How many mouths you got to feed?
How many white folks you got to please
Before you lose your mind?

Can't seem to do enough to please
No white man on this Earth.
You work and work and work and work,
But still you're nothing but dirt.

How many times will he whip your back?
How many times will he call you "Black"?
Don't seem likely he's going to change,
Not less God sends a hurricane
To destroy the white man and his game,
And then he'll blame you for that!

The Insurrection
Vessy Denmark (1767-1822)

Your memory lies within our hearts
Because you had a dream.
Beneath that deep and somber glare
You echoed freedom's scream.

A free man and a carpenter,
You had no cause to spurn,
But freedom for your fellow man
Did cause your heart to burn.

And better yet you had a plan
To free the captive slaves.
To do or die, not asking why,
In hideaway conclaves.

Ten thousand slaves recruited
For that daring slave revolt,
But one among you snared the trap
That triggered Charleston's jolt.

So valiant was your fruitless boon,
A breath from freedom's bliss;
So shameful you stood betrayed
With that well-known Judas kiss.

They captured you one morning
With some thirty other slaves
Who hanged with you on the gallows
To subside that "freedom" crave.

And in your life of valor
You finished one great task:
The men you left in slavery
Will always wear that "freedom" mask!

High On The Hog

Mama used to tell me
How white folks ate "High on the Hog."
The parts of the pig they didn't want,
They fed to the Slaves and the dogs.

Now, the hog was usually the staple of choice,
But white folks ate only the best.
Like the ribs and ham and tenderloin,
And the Slaves were given the rest.

Now the rest, my friend, was not the best.
They ate hog head, tongue and pig ears;
Pig feet, salt pork, hog jowls and brains
Were the staples for many years.

Chitterlings, hog jaws, liver and hearts
Were hardly what white folks ate.
Kidneys, knuckes, pig tails and snouts
Were what black folks found on their plates.

Now, "High on the Hog" meant chops and roast,
Ham and bacon and sausage they fried.
But black folks ate whatever the got,
And that's what kept them alive, my friend,
And that's what kept them alive.

Master

Master, you're drunk again;
You whipped me once before.
How many times you gonna beat me
For stealing that piece of pork?
Don't you remember the whip you used,
The one hanging over the door?
Well, I ain't stole nothing since,
At least not nothing of yours.
Don't hit me with that whip again;
My body is black and blue.
Or I'll have to stand up like a man
And whip the hell out of you.

Jim Crow

Who hung those Jim Crow signs
Along the walls of hate?
Was it the Ku Klux Klan,
The poor white man,
Or the powerful heads of state?
Old Jim Crow loomed its ugly head
And gripped the black man's neck,
With claws of vengeance he devised
To keep black folks in check.

Who passed "separate but equal" laws,
A wolf looking like a sheep?
Defined segregation, inferior education...
Did you think black folks were asleep?
A pencil for you, an old book too,
Get on with your education.
The things you'll learn won't help you much,
Not even in the next generation.

Who passed the Black Code laws
With the fiendish stroke of a pen?
Can't go to public places,
No mixing of the races;
When is this slavery going to end?
That blackbird with his beady eyes
Passed statutes with haste and speed;
Piled laws of vengeance on our heads
To kill the freedom seed.

Who pulled the cotton curtains
Around the Southern voting booths?
How many beans in a jar?
How fast is a shooting star?
How wide is a hound dog's tooth?
That old blackbird devised a way
To kill the colored vote.
With terror and malice,
Drinking from a holy chalice,
Made laws to cut our throats.

Who's going to kill this bird
Of segregation and discrimination?
To restore racial pride this bird must die
By the process of elimination.
This blackbird stole our identity
That was lost in a cruel society.
There will be no more "white supremacy"
As we struggle for our human dignity!

Africa Speaks To America

Has anyone ever asked me
How I felt?
About my children who were swept
Unknowingly from my shores
And taken to a land unknown,
And used in ways absurd...
Without the consent of the Lord!

And yet, you think it strange,
That I should speak of children mine...
Because at your hands they died.
In watery graves they lie...
But the truth shall set you free!
And yet, you ask me...why I moan?
For my children who left home...in bondage!

Your hands of greed made it easy
To capture my children then,
Crushing their souls in the sand
Burying them in your land...
Cutting off their breath,
Destroying the black man...
They could not fight in chains!
You said they had no brains!
And yet...

Understand me clearly now:
When you made my children bow...
Did you think that things would change?
It was a crime, yes you're to blame!
But you haven't found out in all this time...
Putting my people in chains...
What about the ones you maimed?
Because they did not bow,
Who would rather die than be your slave!

Taught them to hate each other,
Made them forget they were brothers...
Stripped of their manhood...
Tarred, feathered and burned,
Castrated with great pain...
Oh, God!...What a shame!

Yes, you had your day...
You had your gain.
Took their language and history
And yes, even their names!
But...

It is important for you to remember
That the first will be the last,
And the last will be the first!
So make way for payment of your deed...
You heard the screaming!
You smelled the stench!

You raped and ravaged the "Black Wench"!
Your heart was cold, your hatred bold!
Understand me again...
These were the works of your hands,
Not mine!

I am Africa!...All civilization started here.
But did I go into your land
And misuse the white man?
No...
Did I put him in bondage or put
Him in chains, sell him on the block,
Kill him with pain?
Did I work him in the broiling hot sun,
Destroy his bones, put him on the run,
Ravage his wife, daughter and mother,
Make him forget his past
And hate each other?

You never feared the God above you...
Because you thought you were God!
Wheeling life and death with the stroke
Of the pen.
Controlling the minds of my black men...
Sapping their blood and burning their flesh!
I nursed your children at my breast...
Yet, you killed mine!
All this will be recorded in the book of time.
Will you be ready to answer this charge?

And still...you look to my shores.
Trying to find ways to explore
My untapped resources of silver and ore.
Eyes on my diamonds, rubies and gold!
But I'm awake now!
I'll sleep no more with two eyes closed.
I'll trust no more your "Christian lie."
I challenge you now! But we will both die...

America! America! Listen, listen to me!
Slavery by any name you choose
Is not a victory!
For when the earth quakes...
We will all go into God's sea.
Unless we learn...unless we know
That the sands of time have run low.
There are no more trips to be made...
And all debts must be paid!
Or we will all end up in that watery grave!

Liberty Lady

I often wonder how things would be,
Proud statued Lady of Liberty,
If you were standing holding high
Your freedom torch against the sky
When slave ships pierced our eastern shores
With men in chains who were free before.
Would you have frowned with great disdain
For wretched deeds so inhumane.
I know that you would scorn such deeds
From men who had no love or creed.

Upon your pedestal you stand,
A tribute to this youthful land.
A monument on the sea of time
With open arms to all mankind.
A state of freedom without fear;
A land that all men can hold dear.
Would you have cried when men in ships
Had freedom only on their lips?
I know that you would not allow
Such fate for humans who had to bow.

You hold your torch of freedom high,
A candescent light up in the sky
Of brotherhood and stars and stripes,
You stand so tall, a beacon light.
A place to welcome every man
You beckon all to this great land.
Would you have shed a wistful tear
For slavery's bondage through the years?
I know that you could not sustain
With men in bondage and in chains.

Upon your head of copper spikes,
A golden crown of freedom's light.
A burst of sunray in your hair
Lets all the world know you are there.
A conquest for the rights of men,
Old Glory flying in the wind.
Would you have hung your head in shame
To see so many bodies maimed!
I know that you would not comply
To see so many humans die.

You stand so tall for all to see,
A harbored haven of security.
The broken shackles around your feet
Support your hate of tyranny.
Your loose robe draped in dignity,
In graceful folds of democracy.
Would you be proud to stand so tall
When black men had no rights at all?
I know that you would not concede
To so much hate and so much greed.

And yet my faith in you is sound;
Nowhere on earth is freedom found.
One nation bold and great and free
With past mistakes, a learning tree.
Where all men have their civil rights
And stand together with their might.
Would you not smile against the sun
To know that race and creed are one?
I know you would be glad to see
All men have pride and dignity!

References

Adams, Russell L., *Great Negroes: Past and Present,* Afro-American Publishing Co. 1969

Bennett, Lerone Jr., *Before the Mayflower,* Penguin Books, 5th Ed.

Blassengame, John W., *The Slave Community,* Oxford University Press 1979

Black History Publication Series, Empak Pub. Co. 1989

Fuller, Edmund, *A Star Pointed North,* Harper & Bros. 1946

Garvey, Marcus A., *The Tragedy of White Justice,* Headstart Books & Crafts, London, England

Genovese, Eugene D., *Roll, Jordan Roll,* Pantheon Books 1974

Gutman, Herbert C., *The Black Family in Slavery & Freedom,* Vintage Books, 1976

King, Martin Luther, *Why We Can't Wait,* Harper & Row 1963

Lester, Julius, *To Be A Slave,* Dial Books NYC 1968

Mannix, Daniel P./Cowley, Malcolm, *Black Cargo,* Viking Press 1962

Rawick, George P., *From Sundown to Sunup,* Greenwood Pub. 1972

Rogers, J.A., *Your History From Beginning of Time to the Present,* Black Classic Press 1983

Stampp, Kenneth M., *The Peculiar Institution,* Vintage Books 1956

Walker, Margaret Walker, *Jubilee,* Bantam Books 1972ed

Woodward, C. Vann, *The Strange Career of Jim Crow,* Oxford University Press 1974ed.

About the Author

BEATRICE GARRETT, was born in Freeport, Long Island, New York. She graduated from Germantown High School in Philadelphia, enlisted in the Women's Army Corps and wrote a weekly column, "WAC-YAK" in the WAC NEWSPAPER. For two years she worked for BLACK HOLLYWOOD MAGAZINE, then opened a Soul Food Cafe in the Skid Row area of Los Angeles and wrote a novel—WELFARE ON SKID ROW—from her experiences there. She has won several awards in creative writing and poetry and was one of the winners in the 1988 Clark College Creative Writing Contest. She is listed in WHO'S WHO IN U.S. WRITERS, EDITORS AND POETS 1986-1987. Ms. Garrett lives in Los Angeles, California and is in the process of completing her second book of poetry, "Black Ball in a White Court."